JUST PRAY ABOUT IT!

The Power to Overcome

By Dr. Marcia E. Theadford

Just Pray About It! The Power to Overcome

Copyright © 2018 Dr. Marcia Theadford

Printed in the United States of America

First Printing, 2018

ISBN 978-0-692-85129-6

Sparkle Publishing Company

www.sparklepublishing.net

All biblical references are used from New American Standard Bible (NASB) and New Living Translation (NLT) ©

TABLE OF CONTENTS

ACKNOWLEDGEMENTS vii

PREFACE 1

FOREWORD 5

INTRODUCTION 7

IMPORTANCE OF PRAYER 15

BIBLICAL UNDERSTANDING OF PRAYER 25

GREATEST CHALLENGE TO PRAYER 35

INTERCESSORY PRAYER 43

PRAYER WALKING 55

CLOSING PRAYER 65

APPENDIX 67

COMFORT PRAYER 69

FINANCES PRAYER 77

GRATEFUL PRAYER 83

HEALING JEHOVAH - RAPHA PRAYER 89

IN HIM PRAYER.. 95

RELATIONSHIP PRAYER 101

SALVATION PRAYER 107

PSALM 91 113

PERSONAL PRAYER TESTIMONIALS..................................... 121

    FINANCES BY DEMARCIO WASHINGTON 122

    "GRATEFUL" BY DR. KIMBERLY ELLISON 123

    HEALING TESTIMONY AND PRAYER BY PASTOR SHIRLEY MOSS........................... 125

    "IN HIM" BY REV. ODELL THEADFORD 128

    MAURICE: TESTIMONY OF COMFORT BY DR. MARCIA THEADFORD 130

    POWER OF PRAYER PSALM 91 BY MRS. BRANDY GIBBS........................... 133

    PRAYER IS A RELATIONSHIP BUILDER BY THE REV. DR. JENNIFER CHO 135

    SALVATION BY BISHOP WILLIAM SURITA 137

ABOUT THE AUTHOR... 141

"Prayer does not fit us for the greater work; prayer is the greater work."

Oswald Chambers

ACKNOWLEDGEMENTS

Always in adoration, I thank God, my Lord and Savior Jesus Christ, whose Spirit has always embraced me with Agape and birthed in my spirit a passion for prayer. This mini book on prayer and my media prayer series would not have been completed without the prayers and assistance of many wonderful people. I am extremely appreciative to Minister Ian Shelly Holmes II, for composing the music to my prayers; El Shaddai Bethlehem "Real Studio" ministry for recording my prayers; Pastor Michael Chase Ridge of ALPHA Productions for creating the visual graphics and for his photographic eye and blessing me with my book cover shot, including Michael Lambert and Virtuous Photography TX for my outside marketing photos. Special thanks to Dr. Jennifer Cho, Brandi Gibbs, Pastor Shirley Moss, Bishop Surita, Rev. Odell Theadford and Demarcio Washington for adding their personal prayer testimonies, and to my dear friend for *always* saying yes, Dr. Sharon Gavin-Levy for writing the foreword to this manuscript. Last, but certainly not least, Dr. Kimberly Ellison for believing in me, encouraging me and coaching me as I navigated my way through this journey and for adding her personal testimony to this manuscript. You truly are my "Intergenerational" G.L.A.M. Squad - Kingdom Boss Chick!

Lovingly, I share this celebration with my husband, Rev. Odell B. Theadford, my sons and grandchildren for believing in the call of God on my life and loving me through this journey. Their support has been AMAZING! I dare not leave out these two beautiful and powerful prayer warriors from this manuscript: my mama, Bettie Joan Kelley-Jones-Crayton, and my grandmother, Alice Williams-Kelley-Gray, lovingly called "Mama Kelley." Thank you for pouring into me the "melody of a powerful prayer life."

PREFACE

The "WHY" of this Journey

"Trust in the Lord with all your heart and do not lean on your own understanding. In all your ways acknowledge Him and He will make your paths straight."

Proverbs 3:5-6

A number of times, I have asked myself, "Why am I writing this mini prayer book?" Although I have taught on the subject of prayer, ministered in churches, written articles and theological treatises regarding the efficacy of prayer, why now have I decided to write a mini book on prayer? Yes, I love to pray. Yes, I love being in the midst of powerful, praying people. Most definitely, I believe in the power of prayer.

Throughout my life, people have always asked me to pray. I pray for strangers on the street, in grocery stores, upscale and not so upscale restaurants. I pray just about everywhere and for just about anyone. My heart cry has always been to make people feel better after they have left my presence and to assure them of God's love. **I am an Intercessor**. Partnering in prayer with God on the behalf of others takes me to a place in the spiritual realm where everything that was hindering the people of God on earth is demolished and prayers are passionately placed before the King of Kings and the Lord of Lords.

"Okay, back to why I wrote this book."

It began when the Lord pressed in my spirit to write a prayer of Salvation. I obeyed. Needless to say, He asked me to write another one, then another one, then another one. Now eight prayers have been written, one of them, my husband wrote entitled "Relationships." Of course, God wasn't finished with my assignment. Next, he wanted me to share them with individuals. I guess this is what our Lord meant when He said, "Go into all the world...with the Gospel" (Matthew 28:19; Mark 16:15). Therefore, I decided to record the prayers, contract someone to write the music for each prayer and individuals to put together graphics for a video for each of the prayers. Next, of course, was to write a mini book to accompany the prayers. Wow! Really, God! If God had told me initially that I was going to do ALL of this, I would have gone back to bed and pulled the covers over my head or binged on a television series. However, I'm glad I submitted to the Lord's will and not mine. God often takes us out of our comfort zone and leads us on a journey that will refine and shape us to fulfill our destiny.

I am in awe that God has entrusted me with this assignment. This journey has not been an intellectual exercise theorizing the existence of God in my life, but about an awesome God who trusted and called me to share His love with others. This book is about the importance of prayer and partnering with God and others in intercession for our nation. I pray that as you study the scriptures, your spirit will be energized, and that you will boldly began to declare the promise of God over your life and the lives of others. As you study God's word, you will begin to know His voice and the voice of a stranger you will not follow. I have included blank pages for you to write out what you hear the "Spirit of the Lord" saying. It will aid you in every area of your life. We are in partnership with the Kingdom of God.

Being lazy is not an option in a partnership. As you read and work through these pages, reflect on the scriptures, meditate on the promises of God regarding your situation and write out your prayer concerns. Place yourself in the text and allow the Holy Spirit to stir your faith in God's word. Here are four things to look for that will help you as you seek God's wisdom in your prayer request. Look for important:

- Learning Moments
- Life Examples

- God's Promises

- Revelations

In the Appendix, I have shared my process of writing prayers, from researching the scriptures to finally putting pen to paper. I pray this will strengthen your faith and give you the arsenal you need to overcome everything that is hindering you from receiving God's best for your life.

I pray that your heart will be assured in God's agape for you and His ability to do anything you can imagine or think. Always remember, "God is our refuge and strength, a very present help in trouble" (Psalm 46:1). All you need to do is "**Just Pray About It**, remember, prayer is the power weapon we use to overcome every attack of the enemy. Prayer releases the spirit of victory in your life and in the lives of those who you place in the spiritual realm before the King of Kings and the Lord of Lords!

FOREWORD

By Dr. Sharon Gavin Levy, PhD

Having a sister friend is a blessing, but having a sister friend who ministers the Word of God and prays with passion is marvelous. Dr. Marcia E. Theadford is a gift to the Kingdom of God and a gift to me. I remember when we met twenty-two years ago; we definitely had some genuine misconceptions about each other. Little did we know, God would remove the scales from our eyes and birth a friendship and sisterhood rich in love, unity, loyalty and transparency. I am indeed honored that my sister gifted me the opportunity to "roll out the red carpet" as she enters this next phase of ministry with JUST PRAY ABOUT IT! The Power to Overcome.

Dr. Marcia is a real powerhouse in this book, motivating God's people to pray. And what I love about her mission is this – she challenges and demands us to pray with knowledge, insight and understanding. Her application of God's Word is the foundation of this book as she pushes the reader to encounter God in prayer as never before. JUST PRAY ABOUT IT! The Power to Overcome, is the fruit of the prayer mantle God has placed on her life. She shares her prayer journey, leading us to where a powerful partnership begins. Imagine a partnership with the Most High God!

My sister's vision of this prayer partnership is clear, for she has lived it. JUST PRAY ABOUT IT, is a result of her experience, humility and anointing. As she has surrendered her cares and concerns to God, He has enlightened and empowered her to share with others. Whatever the burden, she points us to the Almighty. She leads us to the place where we too surrender every area of our life to Him. In many ways she reminds us who God is to us and who we are to Him.

Today, we have so much for which we must pray; our home, our family, our community, our nation and our world. In JUST PRAY ABOUT IT, Dr. Marcia shows that prayer is the process that creates change and transforms our hearts, our minds and our situations. So I encourage you to read this book with expectation because it will reveal fresh insights on prayer. Read this book with excitement because it will revitalize your prayer life. Read this book with confidence because it will renew your prayer posture.

I am thankful my sister obeyed the mandate from God to write this book on prayer and you will be too. Dr. Marcia E. Theadford's wisdom challenges you and me to stop worrying, whining, groaning, complaining, and JUST PRAY ABOUT IT!

INTRODUCTION

"And this is the confidence that we have in God, that, if we ask anything according to His will, He hears us. And if we know He hears us, whatsoever we ask, we know that we have the petitions that we desired of Him."

I John 5:14-15

Request for prayers are echoed daily: "Pray for me to find a job. Pray for my family members that they would come to know the Lord. Pray for my neighbor who has been diagnosed with cancer. Pray for our community because crime has increased, and we are afraid." Those types of requests tug on my heart and have me earnestly crying out to God. Equally echoed are questions concerning the efficacy of prayer. Does God answer prayer? Is prayer necessary for God to act on someone's behalf? Again, those types of searching questions tug on my heart and keep me seeking God for an answer.

Prayer is my refuge, a very pleasant place in the center of my heart. When I am lost, prayer acts as my Global Positioning System (GPS) and gently navigates me safely back home. Prayer keeps me connected to God. This connection has guided, strengthened, and helped me to survive victoriously in my life's journey through a life-threatening illness, an early divorce, domestic abuse, and the death of my son and grandchild. Prayer gives me the "shalom" that passes all understanding. For this very reason, my heart's cry is to be used as a witness of God's love, an unwavering commitment to intercede in prayer on the behalf of others and to remain faithful to the prophetic calling of God on my life. I agree with the psalmist, "The Lord has heard my supplication and the Lord will receive my prayers" (Psalm 6:9). This is one of my declaration scriptures.

When I enter into a spiritual position of prayer, I am reminded of the faithfulness of God and the innocence of learning about prayer as a youth. During the summer months, my mother faithfully took me to Texas to visit my grandparents. One of our weekly highlights was going to my grandparents' church, Elm Flats Missionary Baptist Church, on Sundays. During the devotional time, the deacons and deaconesses prayed, welcoming the presence of God into the worship service and asking God to heal the sick and bring spiritual transformation into the lives of the people. Afterward, they sang songs. One song I enjoyed very much was "Walk with Me Lord." This song always had the entire congregation on its feet, singing and clapping to the beat of the music. It reminded me of God's faithfulness and the Lord's everlasting presence.

INTRODUCTION

The words of the song are ingrained in my spirit. When the challenges of life become overwhelming, full of discouragements and disappointments, I pray, and I sing that song. I loved being in church, it was my sanctuary. It was the place where the Holy Spirit was woven into the fabric of my soul and my heart was knitted forever with Jesus. In the Church and in my grandparents' home is where I first learned how to intercede in prayer for others. I remember those precious times when I went to my mother for her guidance regarding one of my many "crazy" life situations. After she listened to hours of my "confused ranting" she always said, "Just pray about it, baby. Hear what God has to say. The Lord will answer you." If my grandmother was in the room, she would start playing the piano and singing all the verses to "Walk with me Lord."

> "Walk with me Lord; walk with me.
> While I'm on this tedious journey Lord, walk with me dear Lord, walk with me.
> Hold my hand Lord; please hold my hand; please hold my hand.
> While I'm on this tedious journey Lord, you got to hold my hand Lord.
> Hear my prayer Lord, hear my prayer.
> While I'm on this tedious journey, hear my prayer."[1]

---

[1] Walk With Me, Lord, Negro Spiritual: arr. By Nolan Williams Jr.

I just wanted a quick solution to my problem. In exasperation, I would shout, "Please, just tell me what I need to do. I don't have time to pray, walk, or wait to hear what the Lord is going to say!" Patiently, they would tell me again to just pray about it and trust God for the answer. Immediately, my grandmother prayed for God to direct my path and bring peace to my soul. After she finished praying, she would say, "Remember, prayer passionately places us in the Lord's Throne Room." Because of the spirit of peace I received from their prayers and spiritual guidance from God, I will never underestimate the effectiveness of prayer.

Reflections & Petitions

What is tugging at your heart? Is it something personal or is it something about someone else? Just Pray About It! Talk with God about your concerns. Remember, prayer passionately places us in the Lord's Throne Room.

Here are a few scriptures of reflection to help build your faith as you prevail in prayer. Look for:

- Learning Moments
- Life Examples
- Promises & Revelations
- Jeremiah 29:12-14a – "Then when you call upon me and come and pray to me, I will hear you. When you search for me, you will find me; if you seek me with all of your heart, I will let you find me, says the Lord…."
- Mark 11:22-24 – Jesus answered them, "Have faith in God. Truly I tell you, if you say to this mountain, 'Be taken up and thrown into the sea,' and if you do not doubt in your heart, but believe that what you say will come to pass, it will be done for you. So, I tell you, whatever you ask for in prayer, believe that you have received it, and it will be yours.
- I John 5:14, 15 – "And this is the boldness which we have toward Him, that, if we ask anything according to His will He hears us. And if we know that He hears us in whatever we ask, we know that we have obtained the requests made of Him."

My Prayer

Dear God, my heart is crying out because:

_____

_____

_____

_____

_____

_____

_____

_____

_____

_____

INTRODUCTION

"Prayer is not asking. Prayer is putting oneself in the hands of God, at His disposition, and listening to His voice in the depth of our hearts."

Mother Teresa

IMPORTANCE OF PRAYER

"Call to Me and I will answer you and tell you great and unsearchable things

you do not know."

Jeremiah 33:3

Prayer, which has powerful and sustaining properties, is the framework of our faith. God reveals Himself in our prayers. He blesses with us with His agape love. He calms our fears and illuminates His Spirit in our daily lives. He created us in His image and gave us the ability to rule and reign on earth (Genesis 1:26-28). In James's epistle, he advises us to "draw near to God and He will draw near to you" (James 4:8). Most importantly, God has given us His love, which was shed abroad by His Spirit. Therefore, we can live and know the true essence of love. God breathed into us the breath of life and we became a living being (Genesis 2:7). Therefore, God's Spirit imparted life and empowered the believer to carry out His will on earth.

Prayer links us to our community when our hearts are committed to a unified purpose. As people partner in prayer, the atmosphere changes the lives of people, and ushers in the presence of God. Samuel Wells, priest and author, affirms this:

As we gather together in worship we become aware that we are in the presence of God. The ability to name the presence of God develops skills that stand in the tradition stretching from wrestling Jacob to the broken bread on Emmaus road. In His name, the presence of God, the community develops the skills of wonder, the virtue of humility, and the notion of God's glory and faithfulness in a tradition that stretches from the pillar of cloud to the Great Commission. At much of the same time we become aware of the presence of one another.[2]

As a community becomes more grounded in prayer, an interconnectedness of purpose is realized, unity is formed, and transformation is revealed. According to Ed Silvoso, evangelist, community developer, and author, "Transformation does not happen in a vacuum. It is brought about by people who have tapped into a 'will' of resolve and a sense of purpose deep and powerful enough to enable them to overcome the ominous and menacing challenges that

---

[2] Samuel Wells, *Improvisation: The Drama of Christian Ethics* (Grand Rapid: Brazos Press, 2004), 82.

stand at its gates like intimidating guardians."[3] Before we can change the spiritual climate over

cities, we must not only have a working knowledge, theorizing its ability to see if God will move

on the behalf of people, but upon an uncompromising trust that God will complete what was

stated in the lives of humanity, for the purpose of establishing the kingdom of God on earth

until the day of Christ Jesus.

---

[3] Ed Silvoso, Transformation: Change the Marketplace and You Change the World (Ventura CA: Regal Books, 2007), 15.

Prayer in Context

Charles Finney, Father of American Revivalism, said, "Effective prayer attains what it seeks. It is a prayer that moves God, affecting its end."[4] The Free Encyclopedia defines effectiveness as "the capability of producing a desired result. When something is deemed effective, it means it has an intended or expected outcome or produces a deep, vivid impression." Through prayer, we have the potential to impact the world with the Glory of God. Potential is defined as the capacity to develop, succeed, or become something. When we pray, our prayers become impactful and contagious. They impregnate everything they reach. Since we are created in the reflection of God, empowered by the Holy Spirit as commissioned witnesses to Jesus' glorified time on earth, we can pray and bring about a possible change in an impossible situation, change that empowers us with the anointing of God to complete great things on earth.

Unquestionably, the term prayer has been defined in a plethora of ways by a diversity of sources, each with its own complexities on the subject. Nevertheless, in the context of this book, prayer is defined as our partnership link with God, a wonderful synergy between the Creator and the created. For it is through times of intimacy with God that change comes into

---

[4] Charles G. Finney, Principles of Prayer (Old Tappan, N.J.: Fleming H. Revell, n.d.; original copyright, The Trustees of Oberlin College, 1908), 170-171.

the lives of people. Spending time in the presence of God is transformative through prayer. Our prayer should be to see God perform miraculous works in us and in our community through His people. When the people of God pray for their community, awesome things will happen. The scriptures clearly affirm the Lord's presence in our partnership of agreement, "Again, truly I tell you, if two of you agree on earth about anything you ask, it will be done for you by my Father in heaven. For where two or three are gathered in my name, I am there among you." (Matthew 18:19-20). Spiritually, we are never alone when we pray. The Holy Spirit partners with us in prayer. He is our 'paraclete' a comforter, counselor, advocate, and intercessor. As recorded in Romans, "In the same way the Spirit also helps our weakness; for we do not know how to pray as we should, but the Spirit Himself intercedes for us with groanings too deep for words; and He who searches the hearts knows what the mind of the Spirit is, because He intercedes for the saints according to the Will of God (Romans 8:26-27). And let's not forget our Lord, Christ Jesus, He is praying for us. He hears us as we pray and speaks to the Father on our behalf, "Jesus Himself is at the right hand of God and is also interceding for us" (Roman 8:34). Remember, you are never alone, God is omnipresent.

Reflections & Petitions

Do you have someone who can partner with you over a troubling situation that is happening in your life or in your community? If you don't have a partner, just pray and ask God to send someone. God is waiting to respond. There is power in partnership. Remember, prayer passionately places us in the Lord's Throne Room.

Here are a few scriptures of reflection to help build your faith as you prevail in prayer.

Look for:

- Learning Moments

- Life Examples

- Promises & Revelations

- Ecclesiastes 4:9-12 – "Two are better than one, because they have a good reward for their toil. For if they fall, one will lift up the other; but woe to one who is alone and falls and does not have another to help. Again, if two lie together, they keep warm; but how can one keep warm alone? And though one might prevail against another, two will withstand one. A threefold cord is not quickly broken."

- Matthew 18:19 – "Again, truly I tell you, if two of you agree on earth about anything you ask, it will be done for you by my Father in heaven. For where two or three are gathered in my name, I am there among them."

- Philippians 1:3-11 – "I thank my God every time I remember you, constantly praying with joy in every one of my prayers from the first day until now. I am confident of this, that the one who began a good work among you will bring it to completion by the day of Jesus Christ. It is right for me to think this way about all of you, because you hold me in your heart for all of you share in God's grace with me, both in my imprisonment and in the defense and confirmation of the Gospel. For God is my witness, how I long for all of you with the compassion of Christ Jesus. And this is my prayer, that your love may overflow more and more with knowledge and full insight to help you to determine what is best, so that in the day of Christ you may be pure and blameless, having produced the harvest of righteousness that comes through Jesus Christ for the glory and praises of God."

My Prayer

Dear God, I need someone to partner with me regarding:

_____

_____

_____

_____

_____

_____

_____

_____

_____

_____

Dear God, we come in a partnership agreement regarding:

_____

_____

_____

_____

_____

_____

_____

_____

_____

_____

_____

_____

"Let gratitude be the pillow upon which you kneel to say your nightly prayer. And let faith be the bridge you build to overcome evil and welcome good." "While one may encounter many defeats, one must not be defeated."

Maya Angelou

BIBLICAL UNDERSTANDING OF PRAYER

"The beginning of wisdom is this: Get wisdom. Though it cost all you have,

get understanding."

Proverbs 4:7

Prayer is an activity without limitations and it reaches into the hearts of mankind. It crosses into every religious practice. It is an act of our faith projected out of the heart of the one who practices prayer. The late Henri Nouwen, theologian and spiritual counselor, spoke of prayer as a movement:

When our mind has become full of the Lord, and when our heart is empty, we can descend with our mind into our heart, that point of our being where there are no divisions or distinctions where we are totally one. In order to move from mind to heart or from unceasing thinking to unceasing prayer, we have to embrace solitude and silence and then find God in the center of our being.[5]

---

[5] Henri Nouwen, with Michael J. Christensen and Rebecca J. Laird, *Spiritual Formation: Following the Movement of the Spirit* (New York: Harper-Collins, 2010), 22.

Although prayer is not limited to the Judeo-Christian faith, prayer is one of the most treasured assets we have as Christians. Furthermore, it is grounded in the belief that the effective, fervent prayer of the righteous will bring about positive results (Gen. 20:17-18; Num. 12:13; Acts 28:8; Matt. 7:7-11; Luke 18:1-8; Phil. 4:6-8).

During the time when Christians scattered throughout other Gentile countries and suffered hardship and persecution, the Apostle James, Christ's brother, in the closing remarks of his letter to the Jewish Christians, reminded them that the prayer of faith is an effective resource for sustaining the strength necessary to endure to the end. In his epistle, he asks questions that illustrate different life situations and then provides answers that show the diverse types of prayer necessary for each case.

Are any among you suffering? They should pray. Are any cheerful? They should sing songs of praise. Are any among you sick? They should call for the elders of the church and have them pray over them, anointing them with oil in the name of the Lord. The prayer of faith will save the sick, and the Lord will raise them up; and anyone who has committed sins will be forgiven.

Therefore, confess your sins to one another, and pray for one another, so that you may be healed. The prayer of the righteous is powerful and effective (James 5:13-16).

Apostle James shared a message that life would bring about many experiences. These experiences range from affliction to cheerfulness. He is reminding us to be steadfast in prayer, regardless of the circumstances that we encounter. He admonishes us to pray from a position of victory over our circumstance, partner in prayer with the saints, stand on the Word of God to sustain us in our faith, and praise God continually until our deliverance becomes manifested in our lives. God is faithful and the prayers of the righteous are effective.

Subsequently, James finishes this passage by referring to one of the Elijah narratives as an example of God's faithfulness in prayer (I Kings18:1-41), "Elijah was a human being like us, and he prayed fervently that it might not rain, and for three years and six months it did not rain on the earth. Then he prayed again, and the heaven gave rain and the earth yielded its harvest." (James 5:17-18). James cites Elijah's experience to support his argument that God listens to and provides solutions for the one who prays in faith.

Unquestionably, because they were devoted to a life of prayer, the saints of the Bible experienced great things and walked in the Creator's purpose. Clearly, prayer was a very important part of the Hebrew heritage. They were disciplined in their fellowship with their Creator. The nation of Israel can trace its morning prayer back to Abraham (Genesis 19:27), their evening prayers were credited to Isaac's servant (Genesis 24:63). During the third-year reign of Jehoiakim king of Judah, Nebuchadnezzar king of Babylon besieged Jerusalem, Daniel prayed three times a day on his knees giving thanks before God (Daniel 6:10).

The saints had confidence that God's presence was with them when they prayed. "The Lord is near all who call upon Him, to all who call upon Him in truth. He will fulfill the desire of those who fear Him; He also will hear their cry and save them" (Psalm 145:18-19). The prophet Isaiah also reaffirms God's promise of answering prayer, "It shall come to pass that before they call, I will answer; and while they are still speaking, I will hear" (Isaiah 65:24).

Nehemiah fasted and prayed before God on behalf of his Jewish brethren who escaped captivity. He needed a revelation from God to direct him. "O Lord let your ear be attentive to the prayer of your servant, and to the prayer of your servants who delight in revering your name. Give success to your servant, and grant him mercy in the sight of this man (Neh. 1:11).

Nehemiah's prayers were answered. The Lord gave him a plan, gave him favor with the king,

and sent partners to assist him in his mission to repair the broken-down walls of Jerusalem,

rebuild people's lives, and restore people's hope (Neh. 2:1-13, 20). God waits in expectation to

move on the behalf of humanity.

Reflections & Petitions

Let us remember to assist with building up the broken pieces in the lives of others.

God's Will is God's Word. What areas in your life need clarification and understanding? Is it your health, your finances, relationships, salvation, or something else? The Word of God brings clarity. "Be diligent to present yourself approved to God, a worker who does not need to be ashamed, rightly dividing the Word of truth" (II Timothy 2:15). Find the scriptures regarding your concerns on healing, salvation, etc. in the Bible. Ask God to reveal His Word, God's Holy Spirit of wisdom, revelation, and knowledge. It is invaluable. May the God of our Lord and Savior Jesus Christ give you the Spirit of wisdom, revelation and knowledge in abundance, that you will know Him better (Ephesians 1:17).

Remember, prayer passionately places us in the Lord's Throne Room.

Here are a few scriptures of reflection to help build your faith as you prevail in prayer.

Look for:

- Learning Moments

- Life Examples

- Promises & Revelations

- **Job 12:13** – "With God are wisdom and strength; He has counsel and understanding."

- **Proverbs 24: 3-7** – "By wisdom a house is built, and by understanding it is established; by knowledge the rooms are filled with all precious and pleasant riches. Wise warriors are mightier than strong ones and those who have knowledge than those who have strength; for by wise guidance you can wage your war, and in abundance of counselors there is victory. Wisdom is too high for fools; in the gate they do not open their mouths."

- **James 1:2- 8** – "My brothers and sisters whenever you face trials of any kind, consider it nothing but joy, because the testing of your faith produces endurance, and let endurance have its full effect, so that you may be mature and complete, lacking nothing. If any of you is lacking in wisdom, ask God, who gives to all generously and ungrudgingly, and it will be given you. But ask in faith, never doubting, for the one who doubts is like a wave of the sea, driven and tossed by the wind for the doubter, being double-minded and unstable in every way, must not expect to receive anything from the Lord."

My Prayer

Dear God, I need your wisdom, understanding, and knowledge. Please reveal to me your Word

concerning:

_____

_____

_____

_____

_____

_____

_____

_____

_____

"I have been driven many times upon my knees by the overwhelming conviction that I had nowhere else to go. My own wisdom and that of all about me seemed insufficient for that day."

Abraham Lincoln

GREATEST CHALLENGE TO PRAYER

"And Jesus came to the disciples and found them sleeping, and said to Peter, "So you men could not keep watch with me for one hour?"

Matthew 26:40; Mark 14:37

What is the greatest challenge of the 21st Century Church? According to Stanley J. Grenz: The Church of Jesus Christ faces many challenges today. Yet, the greatest challenge is not what initially comes to mind, the greatest challenge is not that of urging Christians to speak out on the great social issues of the day or to engage in political action, even though such involvements are crucial. Nor is our greatest challenge that of encouraging each other to be more fervent in evangelizing the world, even though evangelization ought to be of concern to every Christian. **Rather, the greatest challenge facing the church of Jesus Christ today is motivating the people of God to engage in sincere, honest fervent prayer.** [6]

---

[6] Stanley J Grenz, *Prayer: The Cry for The Kingdom* (Grand Rapid: Cambridge, UK: William B. Eerdmans Publishing Company, Revised Edition, 2005), 105.

Jesus rebuked the Pharisees for telling Him to keep His disciples quiet. Jesus replied," If they keep quiet, the stones will cry out." Our resolve should always be, we will not keep quiet. We will praise the Lord. We don't need rocks taking our place in prayer or praise to our Lord. We will engage in sincere, honest fervent prayer! We must pray so lives will be transformed. We must pray so moral character will thrive. We must pray so leadership will walk in wisdom. We must pray so selflessness will abound. We must pray so unity will be embraced. We must pray because God prayed for us to "live life more abundantly" (John 10:10).

If we want the "Shekinah Glory" to consume what we have laid on the altar of God, in prayer, let's adhere to the advice God gave King Solomon, "If my people who are called by My name humble themselves and pray and seek My face and turn from their wicked ways, then I will hear from heaven, will forgive their sin and will heal their land. Now My eyes will be open and My ears attentive to the prayers offered in this place" (2Chronicles 7:14-15).

Reflections & Petitions

Let us not be found "sleeping" when prayer is needed.

How is your prayer life? Have you kept silent and allowed God to hear the "rock" cry, instead of your voice? If the answer is yes, repent. God is so forgiving. He is waiting to hear your voice. He is waiting to respond to your cry. Remember, prayer passionately places us in the Lord's Throne Room.

Here are a few scriptures of reflection to help build your faith as you prevail in prayer.

Look for:

- Learning Moments

- Life Examples

- Promises and Revelations

- **I John 1:9-10** – "If we confess our sins, he who is faithful and just will forgive us our sins and cleanse us from all unrighteousness. If we say that we have not sinned, we make him a liar, and his word is not in us."

- **Luke 18:1-8** – "Then Jesus told them a parable about their need to pray always and not to lose heart. He said," In a certain city there was a judge who neither feared God nor had respect for people. In that city there was a widow who kept coming to him and saying, 'Grant me justice against my opponent.' For a while he refused; but later he said to himself, 'Though I have no fear of God and no respect for anyone, yet because this widow keeps bothering me, I will grant her justice, so that she may not wear me out by continually coming." And the Lord said, "Listen to what the unjust judge says. And will not God grant justice to them. And yet, when the Son of Man comes, will He find faith on earth?"

- **I Thessalonians 5:16-18** – Rejoice always, pray without ceasing, give thanks in all circumstances; for it is the will of God in Christ Jesus for you."

My Prayer

Dear God, please forgive me. I don't want rocks taking the place of my praise for you. I confess my "challenges" before you.

_____

_____

_____

_____

_____

_____

_____

_____

_____

_____

_____

_____

_____

_____

_____

_____

_____

_____

_____

_____

_____

_____

"A Christian community either lives by the intercessory prayers of its members for one another, or the community will be destroyed. I can no longer condemn or hate other Christians for whom I pray, no matter how much trouble they cause me. In intercessory prayer the face that may have been strange and intolerable to me is transformed into the face of one for whom Christ died, the face of a pardoned sinner. That is a blessed discovery for the Christian who is beginning to offer intercessory prayer for others. As far as we are concerned there is no dislike, no personal tension, no disunity or strife that cannot be overcome by intercessory prayer. Intercessory prayer is the purifying bath into which the individual and the community must enter every day."

Dietrich Bonhoeffer

INTERCESSORY PRAYER

"He has delivered us from such a deadly peril, and He will deliver us again. On Him we have set our hope that He will continue to deliver us, as you help us by your prayers. Then many will give thanks on our behalf for the gracious favor granted us in answer to the prayers of many."

II Corinthians 1:10-11

The Bible is full of instances in which individuals, whether patriarchs, prophets, priests, or ordinary people, partner with an extraordinary God in prayer. They petition God for themselves and on the behalf of others. Scripture calls us to pray and intercede for others continually (Ps. 122:6, I Thess. 5:17, Eph.6:18, I Tim. 2:1). Intercessory prayer focuses on the needs of others.

According to the late Lutheran pastor and theologian Dietrich Bonhoeffer, "Intercessory prayer is the purifying bath into which the individual and the fellowship must enter every day.

Through intercession, we not only provide the service of prayer for one another, we also become more like Jesus, who continually intercedes for us before God."[7]

The Christian Church was born through the intercessory prayers of 120 people who partnered together and prayed. When the Holy Spirit descended, the people not only became aware of God, but they became aware of the presence of one another (Acts 1-2). Richard J. Foster, pursuing this further reveals:

Intercession is a way of loving others. When we move from petition to intercession we are shifting our center of gravity from our own needs to the needs and concerns of others. Intercessory Prayer is selfless prayer, even self-giving prayer. In the ongoing work of the kingdom of God, nothing is more important than Intercessory Prayer. It ushers us into the Holy of Holies, where we bow before the deepest mysteries of faith, and one fears to touch the Ark.[8]

---

[7] Dietrich Bonhoeffer, *The Cost of Discipleship* (New York, NY; Touchstone SCM Press Ltd) 158.
[8] Richard J. Foster, *Finding the Heart's True Home* (New York: Harper Collins Publishers Inc., 1992), 33.

This concept may be found in Genesis 18. This discourse between God and Abraham provides an example of an intercessory prayer that positions "oneself between the Righteous Yahweh and the hopeless, destructive, sinful world". When God reveals the plan to destroy the corrupt cities of Sodom and Gomorrah to His friend Abraham (Genesis 8:17-21), Abraham pleads with God not to destroy the cities:

Will you sweep away the righteous with the wicked? What if there are (50…10) righteous people in the city? Will you really sweep it away and not spare the place for the…righteous people in the city? [After Abraham appealed seven times on the cities' behalf] the Lord said, "For the sake of ten righteous, I will not destroy the city." And the Lord went his way, when he had finished speaking to Abraham and Abraham returned to his place (Genesis 18:20-23).

Because of Abraham's prayer of intercession and God's grace, his nephew Lot and his family were found righteous and they were saved from destruction.

Other patriarchs also placed themselves between God and humankind in order to appeal to God's merciful nature. When Moses led the Israelites toward the Promised Land, he was constantly interceding before God on the behalf of a stubborn and disobedient Israel. Specifically, in one of the Exodus narratives, God was extremely angry with Israel because they had made an idol god in the image of a golden calf. He was determined to destroy them. "The Lord said to Moses, I have seen this people, and behold, they are an obstinate people. Now then let Me alone, that My anger may burn against them and that I may destroy them; and I will make of you a great nation" (Exodus 32:9, 10). But once again, Moses reminded the Creator of the original promise made to the patriarchs and God relented (Exodus 32:11-14).

Some may suggest that God showed signs of weakness because He relents, however according to the late theologian Karl Barth it is a sign of greatness:

The fact that God yields to humanity's petitions, changing God's intentions in response to humanity's prayer, is not a sign of weakness. God, in the glory of splendor and might, He willed and yet wills it so. He desires to be the God who has been made flesh in Jesus Christ. Therein lies His glory, His omnipotence. He does not then impair Himself by yielding to our prayer; on the contrary, it is in so doing that He shows this greatness. If God himself wishes to enter into fellowship with humankind and be close to us as a father is to his child, He does not thereby weaken His might. God cannot be greater than He is in Jesus Christ. If God answers our prayer, it is not then only because He listens to us and increases our faith (the efficacy of prayer has sometimes been explained in this manner), but because He is God, Father, Son, and Holy Spirit, God whose word has been made flesh."[9]

At times we associate compromise with weakness and compassion with faintness of heart. Thus, in our finite ability to comprehend the magnitude of Gods character, our minds must turn to the bleeding Christ on the cross. God's omnipotence is shown in God's agape love for humankind and not weakness.

The Apostle Paul in his letter to Timothy exhorts, "that prayers, petitions, intercessions, and thanksgiving be made for everyone" (I Timothy 2:1). Most importantly, intercession is woven into the fabric of Jesus' teaching on prayer (Matthew 6:5-15), when He teaches his disciples to pray for forgiveness of others' sins. Intercession is Christ's great work for

---

[9] Karl Barth, *Prayer, 50th Anniversary Edition* (Westminster: John Knox Press, 2002), 14-15.

humankind (Hebrews 7:24-25). An example of this is Jesus' prayer of intercession before His arrest. In it He prays for the unification of humanity and the declaration of His Divinity:

"My prayer is not for them alone. I pray also for those who will believe in Me through their word; that they all may be one, as You, Father, are in Me, and I in You; that they also may be one in Us, that the world may believe that You sent Me. And the glory which you gave Me I have given them, that they may be one just as We are One; I in them and You in Me; that they may be made perfect in one, and that the world may know that You have sent Me, and have loved them as You have loved Me. Father, I desire that those also whom You gave Me may be with Me where I am, that they may behold My glory which You have given Me; for You loved Me before the foundation of the world. O, righteous Father! The world has not known you, but I have known you; and these have known that you sent me. And I have declared to them your name, and will declare it, that the love with which you loved me may be in them, and I in them" (John 17:20-26).

Consequently, the Lord calls us to express our commitment to the Gospel by our faith in the unity between God and Himself, which includes exhibiting our love toward humanity. Unmistakably, the greatest commandment is "Love the Lord your God with all your heart and with all your soul and with all your strength and with all your mind. This is the first and greatest commandment. And the second is like it; Love your neighbor as yourself" (Matthew 22:37-39; Mark 12:30-31, Luke 10:27). Therefore, we have a Divine responsibility of interceding on the behalf of others.

Reflections & Petitions

Yes, let us remember that we are keepers of humanity. Pray one for another! People are hurting. People are in sin. They need our prayers. Go to God and intercede on their behalf. Remember, prayer passionately places us in the Lord's Throne Room.

Here are a few scriptures of reflection to help build your faith as you prevail in prayer.

Look for:

- Learning Moments

- Life Examples

- Promises and Revelations

- **Numbers 11:1-2** - "Now the people became like those who complain of adversity in the hearing of the Lord; and when the Lord heard it, His anger was kindled, and the fire of the Lord burned among them and consumed some of the outskirts of the camp. The people therefore cried out to Moses, and Moses prayed to the Lord and the fire died out.

- **Luke 22:31-32** - "Simon, Simon, behold, Satan has demanded permission to sift you like wheat; but I have prayed for you, that your faith may not fail; and you, when once you have turned again, strengthen your brothers."

- **James 5:14-16** - "Is anyone among you sick? Then he must call for the elders of the church and they are to pray over him, anointing him with oil in the name of the Lord; and the prayer offered in faith will restore the one who is sick, and the Lord will forgive him. Therefore, confess your sins to one another, and pray for one another so that you may be healed. The effective prayer of a righteous man can accomplish much.

My Prayer

Dear God, I am interceding on behalf of:

_____

_____

_____

_____

_____

They need:

_____

_____

_____

_____

_____

"We are to be SALT to an unseasoned world and light in a

Sea of Darkness."

John M Perkins

PRAYER WALKING

"Go, walk through the length and breadth of the land, for I am giving it to you."

Genesis 13:17

Prayer walking is a form of intercessory prayer that focuses on the needs of the community in which one is praying. Steve Hawthorne and Graham Kendrick define prayer walking as "praying onsite with insight.... It should be regarded as an important strategy in preparation for ministry." [10] Before planting our ministry, Agape Christian Center, in downtown Easton, Pennsylvania, we prayed and walked through the community. We were seeking God's guidance for the community and declaring every area under the Lord's control. We were following the command the Lord gives to Abram in Genesis 13:17; "Rise up, walk through the length and the breadth of the land for I will give it to you." Prayer walking gets us out of the church building and into the community to pray. When we leave the church and pray in the community, we will get a better understanding of our geographical place of ministry. We must not get so focused

---

[10] Steven Hawthorne and Graham Kendrick, *Prayer Walking: Praying on Site With Insight*. (Orlando: Creation House, 1993), 12.

on praying for our church that we forget to pray for our community. Our church is not an island outside of the community but a living organism within the community.

When Joshua, Moses' successor, was given the responsibility of leading the Israelites into the Promised Land, God reaffirmed His promise, "Every place that the sole of your foot will tread upon, I have given to you, as I promised to Moses" (Joshua 1:3). We share in that promise and when we march forth laying claim to our community we will be victorious. We will conquer the things that have been bombarding God's people. We have the promise of the continued, unbroken presence and rest of God. The book of Joshua gives a powerful illustration how walking around a city can lead to victory:

"Now Jericho was shut up inside and out because of the Israelites; no one came out and no one went in. The Lord said to Joshua, "See, I have handed Jericho over to you, along with its king and soldiers. You shall march around the city, all the warriors circling the city once. Thus, you shall do for six days, with seven priests bearing seven trumpets of rams' horns before the ark. On the seventh day you shall march around the city seven times, the priest blowing the trumpets. When they make a long blast with the ram's horn, as soon as you hear the sound of the trumpet, then all the people shall shout with a great shout and the wall of the city will fall down flat, and all the people shall charge straight ahead" (Joshua 6:1-5).

However, prayer walking is not a free for all. Theologian C. Peter Wagner says, "The purpose of prayer walking is to mobilize a massive amount of intercessory prayer for the neighborhood as possible."[11] It is an organized method of specific prayer objectives. Organizers often target the perimeter of the city as a starting point. They walk the length and the breadth of the city to establish the outer perimeter and then begin to penetrate and saturate every street within the perimeter. As the perimeter is canvassed and the streets are soaked in prayer, breakthrough is imminent. They find that the walls of resistance to the Gospel begin to crumble. The prayers are filled with faith, expecting God to improve and protect the community and its citizens. Through prayer, we have the potential to impact our community for the Glory of God. When we pray for our community our prayer becomes inclusive instead of exclusive. To experience the genuine movement of God prayer must be offered for every aspect of the community. On

---

[11] C. Peter Wagner, Churches That Prays (Ventura, CA: Regal Books, 1993), 182-183.

a mission of kingdom building, Jesus made use of a similar technique when He partnered His disciples together and sent them ahead to every town and place where He was about to go:

"Now after this the Lord appointed seventy others, and sent them in pairs ahead of Him to every city and place where He Himself was going to come. And He was saying to them, "The harvest is plentiful, but the laborers are few; therefore, beseech the Lord of the harvest to send out laborers into His harvest. Go; behold, I send you out as lambs in the midst of wolves. Carry no money belt, no bag, and no shoes; and greet no one on the way. Whatever house you enter, first say, 'Peace be to this house.' If a man of peace is there, your peace will rest on him; but if not, it will return to you. Stay in that house, eating and drinking what they give you; for the laborer is worthy of his wages. Do not keep moving from house to house. Whatever city you enter, and they receive you, eat what is set before you; and heal those in it who are sick, and say to them, 'The kingdom of God has come near to you.' But whatever city you enter, and they do not receive you, go out into its streets and say, 'Even the dust of your city which clings to our feet we wipe off in protest against you; yet be sure of this, that the kingdom of God has come near" (Luke 10:1-11).

When Jesus sends out seventy of his followers into various cities, he tells them what to pray first, and then gives them a specific strategy to follow. Whenever there is a decision to organize a prayer walk, the first thing that must be done is to pray that God will send laborers to go into the field. Next, there must be a well thought out strategic plan. These things are essential for success. This strategy must be unique to your community. It must consider the city's history, leadership, economy, and the problems and challenges within the community. Furthermore, the objective is to focus on seven areas of the local community.

Prayer is offered for the local government, the educational system, the civil organization and emergency responders, local families, local businesses, local media and the local body of believers. When a prayer group concentrates on these areas, it places the entire community under the blanket of prayer. As 21st century disciples, our prayer must be focused on the movement of God's power and not on the fulfillment of our desires. "For the kingdom of God is not in word, but in power" (I Corinthians 4:20).

Reflections & Petitions

Let us "rise and walk," claiming each step for the Kingdom of God. It's time to claim the nation for God. It's time to declare and decree deliverance for your communities. It's time to walk and pray through your neighborhoods. It's time to spread layers of prayers over your cities. It's TIME TO ACT NOW! Remember, prayer passionately places us in the Lord's Throne Room.

Here are a few scriptures of reflection to help build your faith as you prevail in prayer. Look for:

- Learning Moments
- Life Examples
- Promises Revelations
- **Genesis 13:17** – "Arise, walk about the land through its length and breadth; for I will give it to you."
- **Jeremiah 29:7** – Seek the welfare of the city where I have sent you into exile, and pray to the Lord on its behalf; for in its welfare you will have welfare."
- **Matthew 28:19-20** - "Go therefore and make disciples of all nations, baptizing them in the name of the Father and the Son and the Holy Spirit, teaching them to observe all that I commanded you; and lo, I am with you always, even to the end of this age."

My Prayer

Dear God, I purpose in my heart to pray and walk in the community of:

_____

_____

_____

_____

_____

_____

_____

_____

_____

_____

_____

_____

I will claim this community for the Kingdom of God. Help me see the problems I don't see.

These are the concerns I see.

_____

_____

_____

_____

I have strong faith, however when it comes to witnessing, I feel a little inadequate in the

following areas:

_____

_____

_____

_____

_____

_____

_____

My Heart Cries Out to the Lord for YOU!

Prayer will have a positive impact on our lives, our communities, and our nation. Future generations are depending on us to make it right, but it's up to us to pray. I pray, this book and my media prayer series has stirred your spirit and revitalized the power residing on the inside of you. Don't allow it to lay dormant in the crevices of fear, procrastination, or lack of knowledge. As my mama and grandmother always said, "Use what God gave you baby; prayer has power!"

CLOSING PRAYER

Dear Heavenly Father, as we constantly seek Your wisdom, patience, strength, and faithfulness, my prayer is that we stay true and stand strong in our creativity and boldness to the vision which you, Lord, have placed in our hearts. We pray not to become weary in well doing and God provides us with the right people to help cast the vision. Help us to recognize our place in the life of the communities we serve and let us remember to embrace the concept of Christian partnerships, rather than competition and banter. Help us to utilize every resource you have so richly provided for us, without limitation.

May we be distributors of encouragement in our giving, as well as, in our receiving of your greatness. Most importantly, may our hearts be committed to establishing a real presence in this world through our ministries of prayer, evangelism, hospitality, and being witnesses of the Gospel (Acts1:8). May our prayer intensify in its purpose to love and worship God, to demonstrate the love of God to everyone, to unite the lost to Christ, to establish the believer in the faith, and to empower and engage believers for ministry.

We purposely desire to partner with others on this journey of life to bring about a radical change in every sphere of influence, you have designated for us to travel. Thank you, God, for answering prayers and for the Holy Spirit's continued presence in the lives of humanity for the purpose of building the kingdom of Heaven in the earth.

In Jesus Name, Amen and Amen!

APPENDIX

Prayers from "Just Pray About It" Media Series.

The Process

God pressed upon my heart to write these prayers, however, before putting pen to paper, I researched scripture to learn more about what the Word of God revealed to me regarding these topics. Next, I prayed for direction and guidance. Now, I am sharing them with you. Please read and study the scriptures that are associated with each prayer. Ask God to write on the tablet of your heart, so you can transfer your prayers, first to paper, then to humanity. I believe in you! Most importantly, God believes in you and He trusts you with carrying out His Word. If He didn't, you would not have read this book. In addition, I asked seven of my dearest friends to write their "personal prayer testimony." My prayer is that you will be encouraged and blessed by them. Truly, the effective prayers of the righteous avails much.

"Blessed be the God, the Father our Lord Jesus Christ, the Father of mercies, and the God of all comfort, who comforts us in our tribulation, that we may be able to comfort those who are in any trouble by the comfort with which we ourselves are comforted by God" (II Corinthians 1:3-4).

1. *Comfort*

2. *Finances*

3. *Grateful*

4. *Healing*

5. *In Him*

6. *Psalm 91*

7. *Relationship*

8. *Salvation*

COMFORT PRAYER

Dr. Marcia Theadford

"Blessed be God, the Father of our Lord Jesus Christ, the Father of mercies, and the God of all comfort, who comforts us in all our tribulation, that we may be able to comfort those who are in any trouble by the comfort with which we ourselves are comforted by God."

2 Cor. 1:3-4

Our Heavenly Father, the God of all comfort, who comforts us in all our tribulation, that we may be able to comfort those who are in any trouble, by the comfort with which we ourselves are comforted by Your Love. Thank You for Your agape that has been shed abroad by Your Holy Spirit.

Father God, we come to You this day lifting up those who have suffered loss and are going through the process of grief. We lift up before Your throne those who are oppressed, downtrodden, bruised, saddened, or crushed by something that has painfully ended in their lives. Whether it was a loss of a loved one, the ending of a relationship, or the erosion of a livelihood. Yes, we place it all on Your altar. Lord, we are very thankful for the people You have

69

sent to comfort us during our times of grief. We appreciate their kind words, the times they sat with us, cried with us and held us through those painful days. But right now, Lord, we need You. We are "still stuck" and there are remnants of us still residing in each stage of grief. We are trying to move completely from denial, anger, bargaining, and depression to peaceful acceptance. We need Your Peace that passes all understanding and Your Balm that covers and soothes our pain.

Your Word says in John 1:4-5, "In Christ was life, and that life was the Light of mankind. The Light shines in the darkness, and the darkness has not overcome it." We are in a place of darkness and we need the Light of Christ to shine in and through us. We need it to penetrate in every crevice of our soul.

Dear God, we know that You are the only one that can revive us again, our faith rest in You, our Alpha and Omega. You are the One that can heal our broken heartedness and bind up our wounds. You are the one who can restore our crushed spirit. You are the one who refreshes us with Your spring water of life. Instead of allowing our feelings of hurt and betrayal to take over our lives, we surrender and lay it all at Your feet.

We acknowledge that our pain has happened and the emotions we are experiencing are real, but we are determined, by the mercy of our Lord, in the Name that is above all names, Jesus Christ, to surrender our pain, our heartbreak, our sadness, our confusion, our depression, our grief and our sorrow up to You. We raise our hands in worship to You, we embrace Your love, we allow Your Shalom to consume us. You are the true and Living God. We lend and depend on You. We bow before the God that is able to keep us from stumbling, the God that will never leave us or forsake us, the God that feels our pain, and knows our losses and weeps with us; that walks through the shadow of death with us and wipes away every tear.

According to Your Word, we will think and declare on those things that are true, those things that are honorable, those things that are just, those things that are pure, those things that are pleasing, and those things that are commendable over our lives. (Phil.4:8) God, You are worthy of praise. Because of Your love for us, we are able to live, move and have our being in You.

Therefore, we speak against every demonic spirit that tells us we will never recover, or we will never be whole, or complete again from our lost. Satan, you are a liar and the truth is not in you. We cast down every spirit that comes against the knowledge of who we are and the victory we have in Christ Jesus. Only God has rule and reign over our lives. He is Truth. He tells us that we are overcomers because of His blood that was shed and the words of our testimony.

Thank You Lord for sending Your Holy Spirit to empower and comfort us. Thank you Lord for being our refuge and our strength, and a very present help in times of our need. We worship You, King of Kings and Lord of Lords.

In Jesus Name, Amen, Amen!

Here are a few scriptures of reflection to help build your faith as you prevail in prayer.

Look for:

- Learning Moments

- Life Examples

- Promises and Revelations

Scripture References

Ps. 34:18

Ps. 46

Phil.4:8

John 11:35

Acts 17:28

Phil.4:8

Hebrews 13:5

2 Cor. 1:3-4

Rev. 22:13, 1:8, 21: 6-7

Rev. 21:6-7

The Spirit of the Lord is speaking:

_____

_____

_____

_____

_____

_____

_____

_____

_____

_____

_____

FINANCES PRAYER

Heavenly Father, we come together in agreement in the wonderful and powerful name of Jesus Christ.

We thank You Lord, for all that you are doing in our lives. Help us to remember your Word regarding our livelihood and help us to stay firm and not to worry about our finances. Help us to remember that you are the Author and Finisher of our faith. Help us to keep things in perspective regarding your Divine priority.

You told us in your Word, "No one can serve two masters, either they will hate one and love the other, or be loyal to one and despise the other. You cannot serve God and riches!" Therefore, children of the most High God, the Lord says, "Stop worrying about your life what you will eat or what you will drink nor about your body because your Heavenly Father, has everything under control as to what you will wear. Life is more than food, isn't it, and the body more than clothing? Look at the birds in the sky. They don't plant or harvest or gather food into barns, and yet your heavenly Father feeds them. You are more valuable than they are, aren't you? Can any of you add a single hour to the length of your life by worrying? And why do you worry about clothes? Consider the lilies in the field and how they grow. They don't work or spin yarn, but I tell you that not even Solomon in all of his splendor was clothed like one of them. Now, if that is the way God clothes the grass in the field, which is alive today and thrown into an oven tomorrow, won't he clothe you much better, you who have little faith? So don't ever worry by saying, 'What are we going to eat?' or 'What we are going to drink? Or 'What are we going to wear?' because it is the unbelievers who are eager for all those things. Surely, your heavenly Father knows that you need all of them! But first be concerned about God's kingdom and His righteousness, and all of these things will be provided to you as well. So never worry about tomorrow, because tomorrow will worry about itself" (ISV Matthew 6:24-34).

Lord, we thank you for peace that passes all understanding and for keeping our hearts in Christ Jesus. We decree and declare your promises over our life. We will have financial breakthrough in our lives. We will seek you first in every area of our lives. We will rest in your wisdom, revelation, and knowledge about what we should and should not do. We will walk in the path that you have prepared for us. We will listen to your voice for direction. We will not worry about our finances, because you said in Philippians 4:19, that you will supply all our needs according to your riches in Christ Jesus. You are God and you are the One who makes all grace and every favor and earthly blessings come to us in abundance, therefore, we are always and in all circumstances, furnished in abundance for every good work. We will not be "stingy" in our giving. Your Word is true, "As we give it will be given unto us, good measure, pressed down, shaken together, and running over, shall people give unto your bosom. For with the same measure that we give, it shall be measured to us again and again... overflowing." Yes, Lord, it is You, Father that gives us wealth so that we can establish your covenant on earth. We will be a blessing to others.

Thank you, Lord, for your goodness and your mercy. We love You. Amen, in Jesus name!

Scriptures regarding Finances & Money

Here are a few scriptures of reflection to help build your faith as you prevail in prayer.

Look for:

- Learning Moments

- Life Examples

- Promises and Revelations

  Deuteronomy 16:17

  Proverbs 3: 9-10, 10:22, 13:22, 21:20, 22:7

  Jeremiah 17: 7-8

  Malachi 3:8-10

  Luke 6:38, 12:15, 16:11, 21:1-4

  Philippians 4:19

  2 Corinthians 9:8

  1 Timothy 5:8, 6:10-11

  Hebrews 13:5

The Spirit of the Lord is speaking:

_____

_____

_____

_____

_____

_____

_____

_____

_____

_____

_____

_____

JUST PRAY ABOUT IT!

_____

_____

_____

_____

_____

_____

_____

_____

_____

_____

_____

_____

GRATEFUL PRAYER

Our Heavenly and Loving Father, You are the God of all creation. All things came into being through You. Apart from You, Lord, nothing came into existence. Thank You for speaking into earth's darkness and declaring "Let there be light!" and light appeared in the earth and darkness could not overthrow it. Thank You for providing your children with everything that we needed before creating us in your likeness.

Thank You for being love and for Your agape that was shed abroad by Your Spirit. Because of Your love we are completely whole. We can keep going on because we are confident that the work You began in us will be complete until the day of Christ Jesus.

Thank You for birthing in us our purpose and empowering us with the ability to carry out Your will on earth. Thank You for leaving Your Heavenly home so we could be witnesses of Your manifested Glory. Thank you for allowing us to be a part of the fullness of Your grace and truth, which came through our Lord Jesus, the only begotten Son.

Thank You for loving us and never giving up on us. While we were jacked-up sinners, You forgave us and sent Your only begotten Son to die for our sins, to heal us from our infirmities, to take on our sicknesses and to make a way for us to be with You in eternity through the shed blood of Christ Jesus.

Thank You, Lord, for making a way, when it seemed in the natural, there was no way to pay our bills or be healed from the abuse of life or to be delivered from Satan's demonic grip in our lives and the lives of our loved ones.

Thank You for being Omnipresent and Omnipotent. Thank You, God, because of Your Sovereignty we are able to do exceeding abundantly all that we can imagine with exceeding joy.

As the psalmist acknowledges in the 23rd Psalm, You are our Shepherd and we shall not want. You make us lie down in green pastures; You lead us beside the still waters, You restore our soul. You lead us in the paths of righteousness for Your name sake. Although at times, we walk through the valley of the shadow of death, we will fear no evil because You are with us and You always will be with Your children. Your rod and Your staff comfort us. You throw us lavish banquets in our honor. Our enemies see just how much You love us. Thank You, Lord, for anointing our heads with oil and having our cups run over with Your blessings. Surely, goodness and mercy shall follow us all the days of our lives. And, yes, we will dwell in the house of the Lord, our God, forever.

We are so grateful that You are the true and living God. Thank You for trusting us to do what You have commissioned us to do as Your humble vessels.

Grateful, grateful, & grateful, yes, we are, our Majestic King of Kings and Lord of Lords. Amen!

Here are a few scriptures of reflection to help build your faith as you prevail in prayer.

Look for:

- Learning Moments

- Life Examples

- Promises and Revelations

Scriptures regarding Gratefulness

I Chronicles 29:13

Psalm 28:7, 30:4, 69:30, 92:1, 95:2; 100, 105:1-2, 107:1, 106:1, 116: 17, 136:26, 105

John 6:11

1 Corinthians 15:27

2 Corinthians 9:15

Ephesians 5:18-20

Philippians 4:6-7

Colossians 3:15-17, 4:2

I Thessalonians 5:18

Revelations 11:17

The Spirit of the Lord is speaking:

_____

_____

_____

_____

_____

_____

_____

_____

_____

_____

_____

_____

_____

_____

_____

_____

_____

_____

_____

_____

_____

_____

_____

_____

_____

HEALING JEHOVAH - RAPHA PRAYER

Great and Holy Father, our Jehovah-Rapha, the God who heals, we gather today to ask for the restoration and healing of Your children. Send Your healing virtues and heal the areas that have been attacked by the enemy and has caused an illness in their bodies. You are the God of our health and of our countenance. In Isaiah 53:4-5, the prophet Isaiah foretold of Your Divinity of Purpose when he penned these words, "Surely, He took up our infirmities and carried our sorrows, yet we considered Him stricken by God, smitten by Him, and afflicted. But He was pierced for our transgressions. He was crushed for our iniquities, the punishment that brought peace was upon Him, and by His wounds, and we are healed."

Lord, Your people are standing in faith on Your Word for the life of Your children and the blessings of health which You procured before You got to Calvary's Cross.

Lord, we know that You are not a respecter of persons and that You are the same yesterday, today, and forever more. Your love and compassion to heal are boundless. When a leper fell on his knees before You and came and asked, "If You are willing, You can make me clean?," You were moved with compassion. You stretched out Your hands and touched him and said, "I am willing; be cleansed." Immediately his leprosy left him and he was cleansed.

Lord, again and again, You displayed Your anointing to heal. Interwoven throughout the bible are recorded occurrences of Your healings. You are never distracted or stopped by the abnormality of the problem. People brought You their sick - even those who were demon possessed - and You healed them.

Lord Jesus, You are the manifested Word of God that dwells among Your people. You are the True Light of humankind, which came into the world and enlightened us with Your Glory; the Glory, as only begotten from the Father, full of grace and truth.

The truth of Your Word inspired a woman with a blood disorder to press her way through the crowds and touch the hem of Your garment. Immediately, she received healing from You. In another instance, one of the synagogue leaders came and asked You to heal his daughter, who was at the point of death. Many had given up on Jairus' daughter, saying that it was too late for her to be restored and that she was already dead. But immediately You reassured the father and said, "Do not be afraid any longer, only believe." Taking the child by the hand, You said to her, "Ta lit ha kum! Little girl, I say to you, arise!" Immediately, the girl got up and began to walk.

In the name of Jesus and through the blood and authority of Jesus Christ, we speak God's Words of divine healing and restoration into the atmosphere. We come against every demonic spirit that is causing sickness in our bodies. We bind its damaging power from operating in the lives of Your children. We send its destructive spirit to the "dry places" where its effects are inoperable. We loose God's anointing to flow through the world and for His Glory to totally saturate the lives of His children.

May Your people receive Your healing virtues and embrace the victory they have in Christ Jesus. We pray that Your people realize the Spirit of Wisdom, Revelation of God and our Lord Jesus Christ has already been given to them. Thank You, Lord, for making provisions for our healing.

Now unto Him who is able to keep us from stumbling and to present us before His Glorious presence without fault and with great joy. In Your Majestic name Jesus, the Christ, Amen!

Yes, Lord, we are healed!

Here are a few scriptures of reflection to help you build your faith as you prevail in prayer. Look for:

- Learning Moments
- Life Examples
- Promises and Revelations

Scriptures Regarding Healing

Deuteronomy 7:15

2 Chronicles 7:14

Psalm 34:19, 103:1-5

Jeremiah 33:6

Isaiah 41:10, 53:5

Matthew 4:23, 8:5-8, 10:8

Mark 1:41, 2:17, Mark 5:34

Luke 12:13

John 12:40

Acts 4:30, 9:34

1 Corinthians 15:43

James 5:15-16

The Spirit of the Lord is speaking:

_____

_____

_____

_____

_____

_____

_____

_____

_____

_____

_____

_____

_____

_____

_____

_____

_____

_____

_____

_____

_____

_____

_____

_____

_____

IN HIM PRAYER

Our Father, which art in Heaven, to Your Glorious Name, Lord, thank You for making a way for us to become a new creation in You. Because of who we are in You, those old things have passed away. Yes, we have become new, part of the chosen generation of royalty, a Holy Nation in Christ Jesus. We will continue to praise & worship You. There is no God like You. You are the True and Living God, the God that called us out of darkness into Your marvelous light. Our Everlasting God, our Father, of who we live and move and have our being in Your glory. We are the branches connected to the True Vine and God the Father, is the Vinedresser. As we are interconnected by Your Spirit, You in us and us in You, we will produce fruit worthy of the Kingdom of God. When Abraham abided in God's Sovereignty, an everlasting covenant of Promise was established, and Abraham became the father of many nations; God blessed Abraham in every area of his life. As we stay connected to Christ, we are Abraham's seed and heirs according to the Promise (Galatians 3:29). God is light and there is no darkness in Him. We, Your people who are called by Your name are complete in Your love. The anointing we receive from You empower us to do Your will on Earth, as it is in Heaven. Lord, replenish us as we continue to shine Your Light of the Gospel to others. Give us the clarity to see with Your eyes. Fine tune our ears to hear what the Spirit of the Lord is saying to us, and edify us with Your boldness to speak Your words. Therefore, what we bind on earth will be bound in Heaven and what we loose on earth will be loosed in Heaven.

Helps us to stay true to the "Greater" things that You have commissioned us to do for Your kingdom on earth. As the Apostle Paul admonished the believers in his letter to the Colossian, he wrote, "Just as You received Christ Jesus as Lord, continue to live your lives in Him, rooted and built upon Him, strengthened in the faith as you were taught, and overflowing with thankfulness."

Lord, we thank You for choosing us and allowing us to abide with You now and for eternity. In Your wonderful and matchless name, Jesus Christ, Amen.

Here are a few scriptures of reflection to help build your faith as you prevail in prayer.

Look for:

- Learning Moments

- Life Examples

- Promises and Revelations

Scriptures Regarding our Identity in Christ Jesus

Genesis 1:27

Jeremiah 1:5

John 1:12

Roman 6:6, 15:7

I Corinthians 6:17

Ephesians 1:5

Colossians 2:9-10, 3 1-3

1 Peter 2:9

1 John 3:1-3

The Spirit of the Lord is speaking:

_____

_____

_____

_____

_____

_____

_____

_____

_____

_____

_____

RELATIONSHIP PRAYER

Our Heavenly Father, I love and adore You. Thank You for giving Your love to me through the death, burial, and resurrection of Jesus Christ. Thank You for Your saving power that saved a wretch like me. Without You, Father I would be nothing. You are my everything. Thank You for calling me into Your family. Father, I praise and worship You for sending Jesus to shed His blood for me and being my sacrificial Lamb. Jesus, thank You for Your obedience to the Father, for without Your obedience I would be lost. I love You for all You have done for me.

Father, I come before You this day to pray for those who are in a relationship. As Your child, I know You hear me and because You hear me You will grant the petition I bring before You today.

Life is too short to allow bitterness and strife to dominate relationships; therefore, I demand where there is bitterness and strife You will break its power to dominate relationships. May they receive God's power of love because they love the Lord God, as Jesus said, "With all your heart, all your soul, all your mind, and all your strength." And may they be able to "love your neighbor as yourself." Father, give them the understanding that there is no commandment greater than these two.

We pray they may consider how to stimulate each other toward love and good works, and to continue to communicate honestly and sincerely, that they be completely humble, gentle, and patient influencing one another in love and making every effort to keep the unity of the Spirit through the bond of peace.

Jesus has shown what love is by laying down His life for us. Lord, give them the courage, strength, and stamina to lay down their lives for one another. Help them to recognize the needs of one another. Give them the compassion to move, the resources to assist, and the wisdom to comprehend the times of need.

Father, I ask that You strengthen this relationship with the bond of unity that is grounded in the power of love, and their relationship would become stronger each day. May mercy, kindness, restraint, and harmony govern their heart and influence their mind so they act accordingly. May their relationship be grounded on biblical principles, broken hearts be healed, and angry thoughts be cleansed by the love of Christ... in whose name I pray, Amen.

Here are a few scriptures of reflection to help build your faith as you prevail in prayer.

Look for:

- Learning Moments

- Life Examples

- Promises and Revelations

Scriptures Regarding Relationships & Marriage

Marriage

Genesis 1:27-28

Proverbs 3:3-413:20, 31:10, 17:17

Song of Solomon 4:9, 8:6-7

Isaiah 54:5

Malachi 2:14-15

John 15:12

1 Corinthians 13:13; 16:14

Ephesians 4:2

1 Peter 4:8

Relationships

Exodus 20:12

Proverbs 13:20

John 15:13

Ephesians 4:2-3

Colossians 3:23

Hebrews 10:24-25

1 Peter 5:6-7

The Spirit of the Lord is speaking:

_____

_____

_____

_____

_____

_____

_____

_____

_____

_____

_____

_____

JUST PRAY ABOUT IT!

_____

_____

_____

_____

_____

_____

_____

_____

_____

_____

_____

_____

SALVATION PRAYER

Heavenly and Gracious Father, we come acknowledging You as God and Lord of All; Our God, who alone deserves our worship.

Lord, today we come lifting up your desire, the desire that all people be saved and come to the knowledge of this very truth, "That whosoever calls on the name of the Lord shall be saved."

Lord we know, "if the Gospel be hidden, it is hidden to those that are perishing, because the enemy of this age has blinded the unbeliever's mind," so they will not comprehend the light and the wisdom of the Gospel that reveals the Glory of Christ.

Lord, thank You for empowering us with Your Word and infusing us with Your anointing. In the Name of Jesus, we bind the demonic spirit operating in the lives of those blinded (our loved ones, family, friends, and even our foes) from receiving Your glorious Gospel. We render its corruptive power, to be ineffective and we curse the root cause, the source that the Enemy has used to blind them, whether it was the loss of a loved one that the Enemy used, a crippling illness, or an abusive situation that happened in their life. Whatever the Enemy used to deceive them, we render its destructive power, barren, right now, in the Name of Jesus. We send that demonic spirit to the dry places, where it will not find rest and will never return to the lives of those who You, Lord, have placed in our hearts. We decree and declare, no longer will the Enemy be successful in keeping them blinded to the saving grace of God.

Lord, we loose Your Spirit of Wisdom, Revelation and Knowledge so Your people can know You better and have the hope You have called them into. We pray the eyes of their understanding be enlightened so they will operate in the anointing You have placed inside of them.

Yes, Lord according to Your Word, we are calling Light to shine into darkness; we are calling Life to be resurrected in their lives. Yes, let it be done on earth as it is in Heaven.

Touch the heart of Your people and reassure them, there is life in Jesus Christ for their loved ones and remind them to praise You, for their loved one's salvation each time You place them in their spirit.

We thank You, Lord, in advance, for each person's salvation and for preparing the way out of darkness into Your marvelous Light.

We give You the praise God, In Jesus Name, Amen and Amen.

Here are a few scriptures of reflection to help build your faith as you prevail in prayer.

Look for:

- Learning Moments

- Life Examples

- Promises and Revelations

Scripture Regarding Salvation

Psalm 62:1

Mark 16:16

Luke 18:27, 19:10

Acts 2:21, 4:12, 16:31

Romans 10:9-10

1Corinthians 6:9-10

Philippians 3:4-11

2 Timothy 1:9

Titus 2:11-15

Hebrew 7:25, 9:28

1 Peter 1: 8-9

2 Peter 3:9

The Spirit of the Lord is speaking:

_____

_____

_____

_____

_____

_____

_____

_____

_____

_____

_____

PSALM 91

Our Holy and Sovereign God, You alone are the true and living God. Thank You for Your agape that was dispersed throughout the universe by Your divine Spirit. Thank You for providing a resting place for us. Because of Your mercy and grace, we can live and move and have our being.

Thank You for allowing us to dwell under Your protective shelter, Most High, and providing a resting place in the presence of your greatness. Lord, we will continuously say, "Almighty God is our refuge and our fortress, our God, in whom we trust."

We are confident that You will save us from the fowler's snare and from all deadly pestilence and for covering us with Your feathers, under Your heavenly wings we will find refuge. Your faithfulness is our shield and rampart.

We will not fear the terror of night or the deadly arrow that flies by day. We will not allow the evil that stalks in the darkness or any plague or disease that tries to destroy us at midday to distract us from worshipping You, Almighty God.

No matter if thousands fall at our side and tens of thousands at our right hand, Your Presence protects us and danger shall not come near us. We will live and not be destroyed. We will see the punishment of the wicked.

Yes Lord, we will continually declare that You are our refuge and we make the Most High our dwelling place, therefore no harm will overtake us and no disaster will come near our homes.

Thank You Lord for commanding Your angels to guard us in all our ways; and for lifting us up in their hands, so nothing will strike against our pathway as we journey to do Your will on earth. Lord, You have empowered us to destroy the powers of lions and serpents, and in the name of Jesus, we will trample the great lion and the serpent.

We love You, Lord because You are God and there is no god that compares to You. Thank You for being our God, for rescuing and protecting us.

We thank You, Almighty God for answering our prayers when we are in trouble and for delivering us. Most importantly, we thank You for honoring us as Your children and making the way of salvation through the shed blood of Jesus Christ. Now we can live eternally with You in Heaven. Grace, peace, and mercy, in Jesus Name, Amen.

Here are a few scriptures of reflection to help build your faith as you prevail in prayer.

Look for:

- Learning Moments

- Life Examples

- Promises and Revelations

Psalm 91 - New American Standard Bible (NASB)

Security of the One Who Trusts in the Lord.

He who dwells in the shelter of the

Most High will abide in the shadow of the Almighty.

[2] I will say to the Lord, "My refuge and my fortress,

My God, in whom I trust!"

[3] For it is He who delivers you from the snare of the trapper

And from the deadly pestilence.

[4] He will cover you with His pinions

And under His wings you may seek refuge;

His faithfulness is a shield and bulwark.

[5] You will not be afraid of the terror by night, Or of the arrow that flies by day;

[6] Of the pestilence that stalks in darkness, Or of the destruction that lays waste at noon.

[7] A thousand may fall at your side

And ten thousand at your right hand,

But it shall not approach you.

[8] You will only look on with your eyes

And see the recompense of the wicked.

⁹ For you have made the LORD, my refuge,

Even the Most High, your dwelling place.

¹⁰ No evil will befall you,

Nor will any plague come near your [c]tent.

¹¹ For He will give His angels charge concerning you,

To guard you in all your ways.

¹² They will bear you up in their hands,

That you do not strike your foot against a stone.

¹³ You will tread upon the lion and cobra,

The young lion and the serpent you will trample down.

¹⁴ "Because he has loved me, therefore I will deliver him;

I will set him *securely* on high, because he has known my name.

¹⁵ "He will call upon me, and I will answer him;

I will be with him in trouble;

I will rescue him and honor him.

¹⁶ "With [f]a long life I will satisfy him

And let him see my salvation."

The Spirit of the Lord is speaking:

_____

_____

_____

_____

_____

_____

_____

_____

_____

_____

_____

_____

_____

_____

_____

_____

_____

_____

_____

_____

_____

_____

_____

_____

_____

_____

PERSONAL PRAYER TESTIMONIALS

"And they overcame him because of the blood of the Lamb and because of word of their testimony; and they have not love their life even when faced with death."

Revelation 12:11

FINANCES

DEMARCIO WASHINGTON

I've never used prayer as a means to ask God for dollars to magically appear in my bank account. Whenever I've been stuck on a financial issue, prayer was the power I used to ask God to guide me. I wrote the prayer in my diary and waited for God's answer. The key for me was writing that prayer only one time, and not thinking about it again. I've never expected a specific time frame for God's response. I've found God always answered when the time was right for me to accept His guidance and act on it. With clear direction provided by God, I was free to do the things necessary to improve my financial position. I've seen in my life that God always answers prayer. It's just a matter of accepting the form of God's answer, taking action, and having faith. It's in my best interest to do so.

"GRATEFUL"

DR. KIMBERLY ELLISON

CEO OF DR. KIMBERLY ELLISON GLOBAL, LLC

"Devote yourselves to prayer, being watchful and thankful."

Colossians 4:2

My life is a testimony to the power of prayer. Growing up as a little girl, I witnessed my mother's consistent, diligent, and powerful prayer life; although I am not exactly sure what she prayed for, I am grateful to have not only observed, but also adopt my mother's posture of prayer. It is because of her constant position of crying out to God that I too, have experienced the power of prayer. I am grateful to God for allowing my journey to put His grace on public display.

I am grateful that He saw fit to bless me as a mother on earth because there was a time in my life that being a mom was a dream and a nightmare. My husband and I had experienced the joy of carrying and expecting our little princess, McCarley Nichole, only to birth her and place her in the core of the earth, rather than in the beautiful crib awaiting her arrival. It was in that valley moment, the faith and trust I always had in the God I always knew had failed me.

I had never experienced such a dark and uncertain place in my life; we were experiencing birth and death at the same time. While we were going through the labor and delivery process of bringing life into the world, we experienced the end of life process. As we laid our angel baby to rest, I struggled with the thought of how my body failed me, how God had failed me and how I failed everyone around me. It was in that valley moment that the spirit of gratefulness overtook my being. I was grateful to experience being a mom, if only for a brief moment on earth, I was grateful that He spared my life during the process, I was grateful to have a God that loved me enough to bless me as a mother of an angel baby in Heaven, but also grant me the honor and privilege of being a mom on earth. Faron and I were blessed to conceive our daughter of "grace" a few months later.

Often times, we experience gratefulness from our place of lack, knowing that prayer will not only change our situation, but also change how we see our situation. In a place where I could not see my way out, God's grace touched me and carried me to my mountaintop season. My husband Faron and I are grateful to be parents on earth to both our son and daughter. Our children remind us of God's grace and we are grateful.

HEALING TESTIMONY AND PRAYER

BY PASTOR SHIRLEY MOSS

"God's Word Life Changing Ministries"

"Your Word I have hidden in my heart that I might not sin against you."

Psalms 119:11

In 2010, I was hit by a pickup truck while walking my dog as I normally did each morning. The driver of the truck was rushing to work and failed to stop at the stop sign. The forceful impact caused me to be thrown into the air, hit the ground and bounce up again. While flying in midair, I remembered Psalms 91:11 which says, *"For He will give His angels charge over you, to keep you in all your ways. In their hands they shall bear you up lest you dash your foot against a stone."*

A few minutes later, the ambulance transported me to the hospital. After several x-rays and scans, I wanted to go home and was released. The scans showed I had a broken ankle, a concussion, and a dislocated and bruised vertebrae. Therapy for my back began immediately following this horrific event. After a little over a month, there was no progress and doctors anticipated full recovery would take several months. As I attended therapy each day, I prayed and thanked God for my healing and stood on what Jesus spoke in Mark 11:23-24. I knew to expect healing, but did not know exactly how it would manifest. However, one night, a lady whom I had never met, came to my home to pray in agreement for her son. Before approaching the Lord about her son, she said the prayer of salvation according to Romans 10:9-10.

Later, I learned the weekend following our meeting; the lady had a massive stroke. About two and a half months later, she was released from the hospital and began therapy. Little did I know, during her prayer visit to my home, she kept my telephone number and by the Lord's leading, she called me. When I answered the phone, her first words to me were, "I apologize for not calling you earlier, as the Lord had told me, but I wanted to tell you now that God showed me an x-ray of your back. When he showed me, He highlighted each of the vertebrae He healed." I was thrilled to hear this and knew it was the Lord because the lady never knew a truck had hit me! I received her message from God and haven't experienced pain or required therapy since that day.

During one of my most challenging and painful moments associated with this event, my physical therapist commented, "I don't know why something like this happened to someone like you." I quickly replied, "It rains on the just and the unjust as the sun rises each day on the saved and unsaved, but we as believers have the One to turn to: Jesus Christ of Nazareth and through this ordeal, He gets the glory.

In Mark 11:23-24, Jesus says, "*I tell you the truth, if anyone says to this mountain, 'Go throw yourself in to the sea,' and does not doubt in his heart but believes that what he says will happen, it will be done for him. Therefore, I tell you whatever you ask for in prayer, believe that you have received it and it will be yours.* "

Because of the Blood covenant that we have with our Father through the shed blood of Jesus Christ, we can stand on His word and live with expectancy that His Word will do exactly as He said. Almighty God has no favorites, so all who are part of the covenant can believe and expect the manifestation of healing just as I did seven years ago.

"IN HIM"

REV. ODELL THEADFORD

1 John 5:20 (KJV) And we know that the Son of God is come, and hath given us an understanding, that we may know him that is true, and we are in him that is true, even in his Son Jesus Christ. This is the true God, and eternal life. Early on in my Christian walk I learned something about salvation that changed my life. What I learned was that I am in Christ. At first, I didn't grasp the magnitude of this truth. But, as I continued to read, study, and meditate on the Word of God, this truth began to be revealed in my spirit and understood by my mind. With this understanding came revelation to the awesome power that rested within me to overcome the weaknesses of my fleshly life. As I purposed to mature, as a Christian, the reality of my life in Christ began to manifest in my attitude, thoughts, decisions, and actions. I am very thankful that God's nature of love and salvation chose me to be in Christ. Knowing this truth and acting upon it has strengthened me tremendously when pain, indecision, heartache, and inner turmoil have dropped in on my life. I serve a magnificent God who invested in me and entrusted me with the knowledge and understanding that He is the one and only true God and the Maker of all things, both in heaven and earth. I am thankful and grateful for all He has done for me

through Christ. Being consistently aware that I am in Christ has aided me when I have to face the attacks of stress and worry. When these attacks come and I turn to Christ in me, the peace that passes all understanding overtakes me as I lean on He who is greater than me. All praises to God, our Father, and His Son, Jesus.

MAURICE: TESTIMONY OF COMFORT

DR. MARCIA THEADFORD

On December 8, 1971, after 36 hours of labor, I gave birth to love. My extremely handsome baby son weighed 12 pounds and 8 ounces. I named him Maurice Antoine. Like most parents, I wanted the best for my baby. Although I was in college, I wanted him close to me. I hired a live- in sitter to watch him while I attended classes. We were inseparable. During my last semester of college, my mother kept him until I finished my internship. Life was good, but it had its challenges. Not only did I become a mother in college, but also a wife. After 13 years of marriage, we decided to divorce. That chapter of my life is a whole different book.

Maurice, or "MO" was a natural born leader, charismatic, generous, and had a fighter's instinct for getting things done. People were drawn to him. He was the type of person that never met a stranger. He was my confidant and my hero. On January of 2005, at the age of 33, my extremely handsome son died from an aneurysm. My love, my hero had died. I completely went into a "survival mode" to get through the next two weeks. I put a "PAUSE" on my grief. By this time, I was remarried with more wonderful sons. I didn't know until the loss of Maurice, it was possible to put grief on hold; not knowing the hold it would later have on me.

My husband and I wanted everything to be perfect for Maurice's home going. Although, I knew I would be reunited with my son in Heaven, it was still painful. Maurice was well known and had a multitude of friends who attended his service and expressed their sympathies for our loss. As a parent, it gave me peace to know that people cared. It surprised me, probably everyone else as well, I held it together as I closed out his house and put his affairs in order.

I returned to work at the college and resumed my studies at the seminary, where I was pursuing another degree in Pastoral Counseling. How funny I thought, I'm the one who needs counseling. For the next 13 years, I kept the pause on my grief, easing through each stage of grief. I weaved in and out of the stages of grief, tiptoeing through denial, anger, bargaining, and depression, but never completely getting to the place of peaceful acceptance.

God allowed me to keep the "pause" on my heart until I was ready to completely embrace His Love from this unbearable pain. I believe, God got sick and tired of being sick and tired of me "tripping" through these stages. He knew I had greatness inside of me and it needed to be shared with others. The Holy Spirit pressed upon me to write prayers. I obeyed and the prayers became a book. With each prayer I wrote, God took me from my place of pain to positioning me in my place of purpose.

Just when I thought I was finished writing the book and my manuscript was at the publishers, God whispered, "There is one more prayer I want you to write." Write a prayer of comfort and add your testimony. I cried while writing and said, "There is no way I am going to write a testimony. I will get someone else to do it." However, God would definitely have His way, as I wrote the prayer and He provided the strength for me to write the testimony.

My dear spiritual sister Hilda Ray confirmed what the Lord had spoken in my spirit. My testimony will bring healing to myself as well as others. They both were RIGHT! My healing began when I started writing my testimony of God's amazing comfort. I have finally reached the stage of peaceful acceptance. This doesn't mean that I won't cry again over my son, but it does mean, I am not on pause any longer! To God Be the Glory...AMEN!

POWER OF PRAYER PSALM 91 (NEW LIVING TRANSLATION)

MRS. BRANDY GIBBS

I was intrigued when my pastor said, "Read Psalm 91 for 21 days straight and your life will forever change." Well who wouldn't want to try that! So, I started reading it every day, but would forget on some days and would have to start all over. I also recorded myself saying it so I could listen to it on the go. I finally achieved reading it 21 days straight and noticed I had memorized the whole Psalm! I still continue to say this Psalm to myself every day and find different meaning in its context. After reading many laws of attraction and self-help books, I realized they are taking God's word and turning it into modern day language. They use words like universe or the divine, but truly they mean God. One thing these books teach, is to be grateful for what you have before you desire to acquire more. They teach about saying thank you, not to be fearful, and to live in the present and not in the past. These are all concepts taught in the Bible. Many years I struggled with, "Well, what do I have to be grateful for?" I lost my husband to a heart attack shortly after my son was born, I struggled to obtain a teaching position after years of mounting school debt, and live in a humble apartment. Reciting this Psalm every morning has allowed me to see the similarities between these self-help books and God's word. All of the concepts taught in these self-help books are all beliefs that God has taught us according to his word. According to Psalm 91, "If you make the Lord your refuge, if you make the Most High your shelter, no evil will conquer you, no plague will come near your home. For He will order his angels to protect you wherever you go." I love how this verse starts out with the word "if", if you make the most high your shelter then God will shelter you from evil and nothing can hurt you. I love how this Psalm helps me think about what I am grateful for in my life. I may have a humble apartment, but I am grateful that I am not one of the people in California that lost their house to a fire, or one of the people who lost a home in one of the massive hurricanes we had in the US. I may have lost my husband, but I am grateful God showed me how much I value my own life. It showed me how fragile life is and how it can be gone in a matter of minutes. I may not have obtained a permanent teaching position, but God continues to give me work and provide food for my family. Thank you, God, for giving me an angel to protect me wherever I go. I know if I continue to be grateful for what I have, God will give me more things to be grateful for. I am now able to find comfort and gratitude amongst the struggle. Psalm 91 ends, "I will reward them with a long life and give them my salvation." Thank you Lord for teaching me and continuing to be my guide and my light.

PRAYER IS A RELATIONSHIP BUILDER

THE REV. DR. JENNIFER CHO, SENIOR PASTOR OF THE BRIDGEWATER UNITED METHODIST CHURCH, NEW JERSEY

"Rejoice always, pray continually, and give thanks in all circumstances; for this is God's will for you in Christ Jesus." (1 Thessalonians 5:16-18) The Bible begins with one powerful statement in Genesis Chapter 1 verse 1: "In the beginning, God created." After having been a disciple of Jesus Christ and serving as an ordained pastor in The United Methodist Church for many years, I have come to believe that in the beginning God created relationships. It was out of God's love every creature was created. When God decided to create human on the 6th day of creation, God said: "Let us create humans in our image, in our likeness." This meant that God created us human beings in God's own image. Therefore, it is right to describe us as God's children - which means God's offspring created in the image of God. God's Spirit lives within us and we continue to enjoy this very special love relationship with our God, the Creator. Prayer is an extension of our relationship with God. First of all, through prayer we come to a deeper love relationship with God who loves us. 1 Thessalonians 5:16 encourage us to "pray continually." This emphasizes the need to be in constant relationship with God in each moment of our lives. Secondly, through prayer we come to a deeper relationship with other people around us. In this sense, prayer brings our vertical relationship with God and our horizontal relationship with others together as one. One powerful metaphor I can think of about prayer is breathing. As human beings, we must breathe in and breathe out continually. Otherwise, we will not be able to sustain our lives. Prayer is a form of breathing in the love of God and breathing out the same of love of God. As we breathe in the love of God, we are taking in the divine love that transforms us as God's healthy and loving children of God. And, as we breathe out the love of God, we are unleashing the love power of God into the world. Indeed, prayer is like breathing in and breathing out the love of God. Through prayer, we inhale and exhale God's transforming love. Prayer changes. It changes us. It also changes the world through us. Prayer creates and re-creates love relationships among all God's children and all around the world.

SALVATION

BISHOP WILLIAM SURITA

One of the most important parts of my life is when I received The Lord Jesus as my personal Savior.

Unfortunately, my experience was a little bit different. I was involved in church and heavily involved with the youth ministry. I knew everything about church. I knew every single program the church offered. I even enjoyed going to camps and revivals with the youth. I realized just because I knew everything about church and church operations; that did not mean I had a personal relationship with God. I never smoked, really never drank, I was a good boy. I enjoy going to retreats and overall, I enjoyed watching all the girls in the church. (Boy, I loved girls- I was Mr. Casanova.) However, that didn't mean I had a personal relationship with God. I loved sports and chased girls. One day, I met a man who showed me it wasn't about what I did or how much I loved the church, but it was about knowing who God was.

He explained to me, just because I knew Him didn't mean I had a relationship with Him. He asked me, if I knew what size shirt he was wearing? I said no. Then he said, "The reason you don't know the answer is because you don't have a relationship with me. You know who I am

JUST PRAY ABOUT IT!

but you don't buy my clothes." That's the same thing with God. Just because you know who He is, doesn't mean that you have a personal relationship. That's when I started to ask more questions? How can I have a personal relationship with Him? How can I know him? How can I feel him? How can I know He is there? Those questions started to increase my love for knowing God. As I started to see Him, that's when things started to change. Even though I was in church, even though I participated in all the activities, it didn't mean that I knew Him. That's the day when I made a major decision and I truly accepted the Lord as my personal savior. I said, "*I need to know who you are and I want to know who you are.*" I wanted to have a relationship with Him. That day, I felt free from everything. I knew I was not the same. That's when I knew I was totally in God's hands. Salvation is a very simple process. Accepting the Lord as your personal Savior is asking for forgiveness, but it is also knowing who He is. You can't accept something you don't know. You can't ask forgiveness unless you're willing to let go. When you know who He is and He's in your heart, everything starts changing.

I also want to add, the power of a praying woman. I had many women praying for me. These were all elderly women, including my mother. They prayed that I would make a decision and totally commit my life to Christ. It was not just a religious experience, but it was a personal experience. Many confuse religious experiences with God experiences.

Once this happened in my life, everything changed. My attitude, my vocabulary, my love for life changed. My love for God was so strong, all I wanted to do was love Him. My salvation experience was very powerful, because it changed everything about me. I pray that if anybody reads this, they realize just because you go to church, just because you feel good when you sing, just because you hear the word once a week or even twice a week, does not mean you have a personal relationship with Almighty God. This was my experience in Salvation.

ABOUT THE AUTHOR

The **Reverend Dr. Marcia Theadford**, ordained since 1995, is no stranger to the Gospel. She holds a Master's degree in Education from **Texas Christian University**, and completed her concentration credits toward a Masters in Pastoral Counseling from **Moravian Theological Seminary** before transferring to **Drew University** where she earned her Doctorate in Ministry, School of Theology. For over thirty years she worked in academia as a Counselor, Professor, and Department administrator.

Her passion and involvement in ministry began at the age of thirteen when she formed a teenage ministry for girls called, ***"I'm a Teenager Lord, Now What!"*** The anointed pastoral mantle placed upon Dr. Marcia and her husband Rev. Odell has broadened their territory and carried them throughout the United States of America. Her unique presentation of the Gospel has enabled her to minister to various denominations and organizations while demonstrating the awesome power of God's love to save, deliver, and set people free from the grips of the enemy. Other ministries have been birthed, such as **"Gathering of Friends Ministry",** a talk show entitled, **"Conversations with Marcia", and "Iron Sharpens Iron,"** a bible study.

Presently, she is the Visionary of the **G.L.A.M. (Godly Ladies Anointed for MORE) SQUAD an Intergenerational Women's Mentoring Ministry**. In addition to ministry work, she and her husband started a successful T-shirt business, **"Tees That Bling & More."** Another entrepreneurial stream is **Mary Kay Cosmetics.**

Family is important, as she is blessed to have six wonderful sons and an awesome array of grandchildren. God and family life are her highest priorities besides being an educator, evangelist, friend, counselor, and mentor. The Lord has strengthened, guided, and helped her to heal victoriously from a crippling illness, an early divorce, domestic abuse, as well as the death of her son and grandchild. These experiences have taught her to **trust God in all things**. Therefore, she is willing and able to assist others in fulfilling their destiny by applying the necessary biblical attributes of wisdom, love, and understanding.

Dr. Marcia cherishes her husband Rev. Odell, as they are indeed one. She reaps the rewarding experience and the awesome power of God's anointing as they minister together. Being of one mind and as vessels ready for the Master's use. They are a team standing on a firm foundation.